by Dr. Randy T. Johnson

with contributions by:

Noble Baird
Holly Boston
Chris Cain
Trevor Cole
Caleb Combs
Carole Combs
Isaiah Combs
Jayson Combs
Brett Eberle
Donna Fox
Danielle Hardenburg
Eric Jeffrey
Debbie Kerr
Wes McCullough
Jill Osmon
Ken Perry
Phil Piasecki
Ryan Story
Katrina Young
Tommy Youngquist

Copyright © 2017 The River Church

All rights reserved. No part of this book may be reproduced or transmitted in any form or by any means, electronic or mechanical, including photocopying, recording or by any information storage and retrieval system, without the written permission of The River Church. Inquiries should be sent to the publisher.

First Edition, October 2017

Published by:
The River Church
8393 E. Holly Rd.
Holly, MI 48442

Scriptures are taken from the Bible,
English Standard Version (ESV)

THE RIVER CHURCH

Printed in the United States of America

Contents

WEEK 1: MIRACULOUS CONCEPTION & BIRTH

- Study Guide ... 7
- Devotion 1: It is Time ... 13
- Devotion 2: Miracle Baby #1 ... 15
- Devotion 3: The Spirit of Elijah ... 17
- Devotion 4: Absolutes ... 19
- Devotion 5: Promise Fulfilled ... 21
- Devotion 6: Trust and Obey ... 23

WEEK 2: MINISTRY

- Study Guide ... 27
- Devotion 1: The Messenger ... 33
- Devotion 2: Repent ... 35
- Devotion 3: Prep Work ... 37
- Devotion 4: A Brood of Vipers ... 39
- Devotion 5: Winnowing Fork ... 43
- Devotion 6: Status No ... 45

WEEK 3: IMPRISONMENT & DOUBT

- Study Guide ... 49
- Devotion 1: I am not the Christ! ... 55
- Devotion 2: Voice of God ... 57
- Devotion 3: True Humility ... 59
- Devotion 4: Doubt ... 61
- Devotion 5: The Red Pill or the Blue one? ... 63
- Devotion 6: Blessed to be a Blessing ... 67

WEEK 4: DEATH

Study Guide **71**
Devotion 1: Prophet vs. Politician **77**
Devotion 2: Prompting **79**
Devotion 3: A Job Well Done **81**
Devotion 4: The Compliment **83**
Devotion 5: Listen to my Mouth **85**
Devotion 6: Swimming Lesson **87**

01 / *Pastor Jayson Combs, Family Pastor*

Miraculous Conception and Birth

Miraculous Conception and Birth

*S*even years ago, I remember receiving a phone call. I was at our Waterford location, and my wife called and said the baby was on the way. I rushed home to get my wife, and we were off to the hospital. Within fifteen minutes of being at the hospital my son was born, my wife did not waste any time. It was an amazing time! I am so grateful for the blessing of my son.

My wife and I have always talked about a having a big family. We were looking forward to making that trip to the hospital a few more times in our lives. Seven years later, there have been no trips to the hospital, and no more babies. As I read the first chapter of Luke, I honestly hope and pray that the Lord is speaking this to me today. Reading this, I seem to feel the pain that Zechariah and Elizabeth felt. In the culture at that time of Jesus, if you did not have a child, you were made to feel less significant than everyone else. Without realizing it, God had something amazing in store for Zechariah and Elizabeth. From the lows to the high, I believe we all can learn a great deal from the parents of John the Baptizer.

> *"5 In the days of Herod, king of Judea, there was a priest named Zechariah, of the division of Abijah. And he had a wife from the daughters of Aaron, and her name was Elizabeth. 6 And they were both righteous before God, walking blamelessly in all the commandments and statutes of the Lord. 7 But they had no child, because Elizabeth was barren, and both were advanced in years.*
>
> *8 Now while he was serving as priest before God when his division was on duty, 9 according to the custom of the priesthood, he was chosen by lot to enter the temple of the Lord and burn incense. 10 And the whole multitude of the people were praying outside at the hour of incense. 11 And there appeared to him an angel of the Lord standing on*

the right side of the altar of incense. 12 And Zechariah was troubled when he saw him, and fear fell upon him. 13 But the angel said to him, "Do not be afraid, Zechariah, for your prayer has been heard, and your wife Elizabeth will bear you a son, and you shall call his name John. 14 And you will have joy and gladness, and many will rejoice at his birth, 15 for he will be great before the Lord. And he must not drink wine or strong drink, and he will be filled with the Holy Spirit, even from his mother's womb. 16 And he will turn many of the children of Israel to the Lord their God, 17 and he will go before him in the spirit and power of Elijah, to turn the hearts of the fathers to the children, and the disobedient to the wisdom of the just, to make ready for the Lord a people prepared."

18 And Zechariah said to the angel, "How shall I know this? For I am an old man, and my wife is advanced in years." 19 And the angel answered him, "I am Gabriel. I stand in the presence of God, and I was sent to speak to you and to bring you this good news. 20 And behold, you will be silent and unable to speak until the day that these things take place, because you did not believe my words, which will be fulfilled in their time." 21 And the people were waiting for Zechariah, and they were wondering at his delay in the temple. 22 And when he came out, he was unable to speak to them, and they realized that he had seen a vision in the temple. And he kept making signs to them and remained mute. 23 And when his time of service was ended, he went to his home.

24 After these days his wife Elizabeth conceived, and for five months she kept herself hidden, saying, 25 "Thus the Lord has done for me in the days when he looked on me, to take away my reproach among people." (Luke 1:5-25)

Miraculous Conception and Birth

What happened to Zechariah in Luke 1:5-17? Who came and visited him? How does Zechariah respond? _____
_____ *Gabriel* _____
_____ *Zechariah responds w/ doubt* _____

What do we learn about Zechariah and Elizabeth's journey in Luke 1:18 and verse 25? _____
_____
_____
_____

What do we learn in Luke 1 about who their son was going to be? Luke 1:16; Luke 1:17; Luke 1:66; Luke 1:76-77 _____
_____
_____
_____

Compare Luke 1:16-17 to the last paragraph in the Old Testament. There is a 400 years gap between these two books. What do you find interesting about this? _____
_____
_____

At the end of Luke 1, after John was born, Zechariah gets a word from the Lord. In verses 78 and 79 it talks about the **"darkness that they are sitting in,"** but the light that is soon to come.

It is encouraging to me that through this low that Zechariah and Elizabeth were experiencing, they were still faithful to their God. Verse 8 says, **"they were both righteous before God, walking blamelessly in all the commandments and statues of the Lord."**

Have you ever felt like there was a time in your life when you did not hear from God? Why did you think that prayer would never be answered? How did you respond to that situation? _____
_____
_____

Have you ever prayed earnestly about something? Did you come to a point that you did not really believe God would ever hear your prayers? _____
_____
_____

I believe this is where Zechariah was. In verse 13, the angel tells him, **"that his prayer has been answered."** Yet, in verse 20 we find that Zechariah could not bring himself to a place to even believe Gabriel. He was praying for something that he did not believe to be possible.

How did Zechariah and Elizabeth react during the birth of their son?
_____
_____
_____

How does Zechariah describe the coming of the future Messiah in Luke 1:78-79? _____
_____
_____

I hope the story of Zechariah and Elizabeth give you courage and strength to stay faithful to God, even when He feels so far away. This story should help even when life seems to be at its lowest, and the words from the people around you hurt. I love knowing my God is faithful and that He gives me the strength that I need.

How can 1 Corinthians 1:7-9 give you encouragement in these situations? _____
_____
_____
_____

Miraculous Conception and Birth / Devotion 1

It is Time

Donna Fox / *Assistant to the Growth Pastor*

> *"In the days of Herod, king of Judea, there was a priest named Zechariah, of the division of Abijah. And he had a wife from the daughters of Aaron, and her name was Elizabeth. And they were both righteous before God, walking blamelessly in all the commandments and statutes of the Lord. But they had no child, because Elizabeth was barren, and both were advanced in years." Luke 1:5-7*

The time had come. Time for things to be put into place for Jesus to come to Earth. God had a plan, a perfect plan (Are not ALL of God's plans perfect?!). Sin was rampant. The one to pay for all mankind's sin was about to come.

The one to announce this miracle would be John the Baptist. The story of John's conception and birth is fascinating. His parents, Zechariah and Elizabeth, were "advanced in years." They had no children and had resigned to the fact they would not have any children.

Have we not all been there? You want something so bad. Time passes, and you do not get it. You are frustrated, feel defeated and hopeless. But these two remained faithful. It is through their faithfulness that God would use them to bear a son, John. John would be the one to announce Jesus' coming and purpose. What an incredible story of how remaining faithful to God will reward you in the end!

They were "righteous," "blameless." They both came from priestly descent. Both were righteous inside and out. Not like some of the other leaders and priests who were hypocrites, putting on an outward appearance that did not match their hearts. These parents-to-be were righteous in God's eyes, not just because of their outward appearance.

The Bible does not tell us much about Zechariah and Elizabeth. But we do know that they were chosen to bear John the Baptist because of their faithfulness, and their age. Friends and family would know that this had to be of God and that this child was special.

Having been barren was a disgrace at this time. It might even appear as a punishment by God, possibly because of sin, or not having God's blessing. But they remained faithful and did not turn away from God. By waiting until they were older, God would show that He is a God of miracles and a God who answers the prayers of the faithful.

God chose this time to fulfill His promise of a redeemer, to use Zechariah and Elizabeth in the plan, to bless them with the child of their dreams, who would go on to baptize Jesus. Their patience was rewarded!

We can be reminded by their story to be faithful because God will remember!

Miraculous Conception and Birth / Devotion 2

Miracle Baby #1

Phil Piasecki / *Worship Leader*

Recently I have been challenged to deepen my prayer life. Mary and I have made it a point to consistently pray for specific things daily, earnestly waiting on God to answer them. Since January 1st there are a few things we have sat down and prayed for every single night, we have seen God answer those prayers in certain ways, and are still waiting on Him to respond to some of the other ones. Previously in my life, I would pray for something for a while, and when I felt like I was not getting an answer, I would stop. For seasons I had stopped praying for salvation for particular people, ceased praying for friends to be able to have children, and the list could continue. I became ashamed of my lack of consistency when I started thinking about the numerous different stories in the Bible of people praying for years for something specific to happen.

The story of the conception of John the Baptist is an incredible example of what our prayer life should look like, and what our daily life should look like while we are waiting for an answer to prayer. Let us look at Luke 1:8-13 to see the incredible example of Zechariah.

> *"Now while he was serving as priest before God when his division was on duty, according to the custom of the priesthood, he was chosen by lot to enter the temple of the Lord and burn incense. And the whole multitude of the people were praying outside at the hour of incense. And there appeared to him an angel of the Lord standing on the right side of the altar of incense. And Zechariah was troubled when he saw him, and fear fell upon him. But the angel said to him, 'Do not be afraid, Zechariah, for your prayer has been heard, and your wife Elizabeth will bear you a son, and you shall call his name John.'"*

We know that Zechariah and Elizabeth had been praying for Elizabeth to be able to get pregnant for a while, she was at the age where the idea of it even happening was laughable. Waiting on an answer to prayer for that long is not an easy thing, but we see that Zechariah continued to live a God-honoring life while he was waiting. It can be so easy for us to get discouraged if we are not getting the answer to prayer from God that we want, and that can cause us to stop living the life God has commanded for us. Some people stop serving the Church because they are disappointed in God, some people stop praying altogether because they feel like God does not hear them, and these are all sinful responses. Zechariah did not let the discouragement of a seemingly unanswered prayer keep him from living a God-honoring life. This Scripture finds Zechariah serving God in the temple, completing his duties as a priest, and worshipping God. In the midst of our waiting on an answer to prayer, we need to take the example of Zechariah to heart and make sure we are continuing to honor God in the midst of our waiting.

When the angel appears to Zechariah, he reassured him that his prayers had been heard, and promises that his wife was going to bear them a son. That must have been such an incredible moment to hear from an angel that God had heard his prayers. We can always pray in confidence knowing that Christ hears our prayers. Even when we may not feel like we are getting answers, we can always know that God hears our every prayer. He wants us to pour out our requests at His feet. If you find yourself discouraged in your prayer life, replace Zechariah's name with your own. God hears your prayers, stay faithful in the midst of your waiting, and expect God to work in incredible ways.

Miraculous Conception and Birth / Devotion 3

The Spirit of Elijah

Pastor Ryan Story / *Student Pastor*

Be honest, have you read the Bible and not understood what something meant? Sadly, we run into those hard verses, and if we did not have Google, we all might be in serious jeopardy. I will admit, preparing to write about John the Baptist I ran into such a verse. Luke 1:17 says that John ***"will go before him (Jesus) in the spirit and power of Elijah."*** Now we all know what John the Baptist did, if not I recommend reading the Bible a bit. John was to prepare the way for Jesus, but when reading this, I ran into ***"in the spirit and power of Elijah."*** Instantly, I paused and let out an unexplainable sound of confusion. What does it mean to have the spirit and power of Elijah? Better yet, how do I take this verse and make it applicable to my life?

John and Elijah had something in common. Now we must not think that John is the reincarnation of Elijah. John himself even dismisses that claim. The spirit that John and Elijah both had in them, was a bold, uncompromising stand for the Word of God. Elijah was willing to stand against King Ahab, Jezebel, and the false prophets of Baal. Elijah never wavered, never backed down, and was willing to say what he needed to say and do what he needed to do to be obedient to God. Likewise, John the Baptist stood up to a Jewish and Roman nation that viewed him more as a madman than an instrument of God. John preached against the self-righteous religious elite. John and Elijah were not always perfect. Both had moments where they questioned God. John's moment came while he was facing his death in a jail cell and Elijah's came by a riverbank facing virtually the same issue. There were moments in both these men's lives where they lost sight of things, but that never took away from the fact that God was still their primary focus.

There are a lot of times in our lives where as Christians we can fall into a stereotypical doormat Christian. Whenever a Christian speaks the truth, it is amazing how often the world will rebuttal with "that was not godly." It can become a scary thing if we become the type of Christian who operates in the safest most non-confrontational way. Now there is a time for meekness and gentleness, but there are times when God's people need to rock the boat. I am not saying to sin while doing this, but there needs to be a point where God's people come out of hiding and be willing to show they live for Him. It is easy to live an undercover Christian lifestyle and just go to church on weekends and no one knows it. We should all be willing to take a page out of John or Elijah's book and be willing to speak the truth (this must be done in love) boldly.

Imagine a nation where all the people who claimed to be living for Jesus turned around and were not afraid to evangelize to their co-workers or fellow students. What would it look like if Christians were bold enough to not act like the world and were willing to take public scrutiny for the sake of Jesus? Imagine the world where men lead their families as they were designed. Imagine the world where teens would be willing to pray before school every day. Imagine the world where we stopped to pray for people who were hurting. A follower of Christ is meant to be bold, is intended to be counter-cultural, and a follower of Christ has no fear in this world.

Miraculous Conception and Birth / Devotion 4

Absolutes

Wes McCullough / *Production Director*

There are absolutes in this world. Matter cannot be created or destroyed. For every action, there is an equal and opposite reaction. Everything that goes up must come down. We do not question these rules because they are known and accepted truths. There is another absolute, the Almighty God is not bound by absolutes, and we can learn from Zechariah that it is not a good idea to be skeptical of God's Word coming from an angel. Zechariah was told in Luke 1:18-23 that he and his wife would have a child. Zechariah was doubtful because his wife was barren and they were now well beyond their child-bearing years. For his lack of faith, Zechariah was made unable to speak until his child was born.

In the book of Matthew, Jesus gives a powerful lesson, ***"If you have faith and do not doubt…if you say to this mountain, 'Be taken up and thrown into the sea,' it will happen"*** (Matthew 21:21). In Matthew 14 we read about Jesus feeding over 5000 people. The Disciples doubted that they could afford to feed the large group that had gathered to listen to Jesus. Jesus stunned them all when His prayer to God turned a small boy's lunch into an abundance for thousands of people. Also in Matthew 14, we read of Jesus walking on water and calling Peter out to Him. Peter successfully walks on water until he is distracted by the wind and waves and begins to sink. Somehow Peter forgot that he was already doing the impossible. These are a few of the countless examples of God's power over the "impossible." Our thinking tends to be limited to what we think is possible when we should remember Matthew 21:22, ***"Whatever you ask in prayer, you will receive, if you have faith."***

Zechariah was a faithful, God-fearing man. He knew God had no limits, but like us, he was distracted by his limitations. For nine months his inability to speak was a daily reminder of the sin and doubt that was in his heart. We need not doubt. God knows the desires of our heart, and we should bring them to Him humbly and honestly. *"Do not be anxious about anything, but in everything by prayer and supplication with thanksgiving let your requests be made known to God. And the peace of God, which surpasses all understanding, will guard your hearts and your minds in Christ Jesus"* (Philippians 4:6-7).

We are all going to face doubt and uncertainties in this life, but one thing is for sure, faith is much stronger than any doubts this world can cause. God has no restrictions and no handicaps. Focus on His power, not your limitations.

> *"Trust in the Lord with all your heart, and do not lean on your own understanding"* (Proverbs 3:5).

Miraculous Conception and Birth / Devotion 5

Promise Fulfilled

Chris Cain

I want what I want, and I want it now. We have all heard that phrase in mainstream song lyrics, out of our children's mouths, and of course on the movie screen spoken by the infamous Veruca Salt. Perhaps you have spoken those words yourself. And are you not glad that you did not get what you wanted when you wanted it? God ALWAYS has a better plan. We call that, "His perfect timing."

We all know how challenging it is waiting and trusting in His perfect timing. All week long you have been reading and studying about Zechariah and Elizabeth. Does God's "perfect timing" have anything to do with them? I mean, after all, Elizabeth was barren, and they were both at least 60 years-old which had meant their time to conceive had expired quite some time ago. Who cares about timing, it is a hopeless situation for sure. Or is it?

> Luke 1:24-25 says, *"After these days his wife Elizabeth conceived, and for five months she kept herself hidden, saying, 'Thus the Lord has done for me in the days when he looked on me, to take away my reproach among people.'"* Verses 57-58 add, *"Now the time came for Elizabeth to give birth, and she bore a son. And her neighbors and relatives heard that the Lord had shown great mercy to her, and they rejoiced with her."*

Wow. Promise fulfilled. The shame, the disgrace, the reproach, and the disappointment has been taken away. God does accomplish His perfect will in His perfect timing and sometimes in very unexpected (perfect) ways. Our God is a God of the impossible. There are thousands of promises in the Bible, and they help carry us through times of support and need. If you are in a difficult season and craning your neck to look ahead, please do not miss out on seeing what God is trying to show you during your time of waiting. Keep praying as Zechariah did. Remember God is faithful. He is true to His people; He is faithful to His Word and faithful to Himself. He is Perfect, each and every time.

Miraculous Conception and Birth / Devotion 6

Trust and Obey

Noble Baird / *Community Center Director*

One of my favorite parts of church gatherings is when we do child dedications. For me, it is so exciting to see parents coming before the congregation to dedicate their child or children, to God. Now, this dedication does not signify the child's walk with Christ or express their faith in Him. However, it is the proclamation before God that the parents of the child will do all they can to surround the child with the love of Christ and to raise them upon godly principles. Likewise, the congregation is charged to help surround the child in a Christ-centered community that will exemplify His love and teachings.

In Luke 1:57-66, we read of the birth and dedication of John the Baptist. Luke writes,

> *"Now the time came for Elizabeth to give birth, and she bore a son. And her neighbors and relative heard that the Lord had shown great mercy to her, and they rejoiced with her. And on the eighth day they came to circumcise the child. And they would have called him Zechariah after his father, but his mother answered, 'No; he shall be called John.' And they said to her, 'None of your relatives is called by this name.' And they made signs to his father, inquiring what he wanted him to be called. And he asked for a writing tablet and wrote, 'His name is John.' And they all wondered. And immediately his mouth was opened and his tongue loosed, and he spoke, blessing God. And fear came on all their neighbors. And all these things were talked about through all the hill country of Judea, and all who heard them laid them up in their hearts, saying, 'What then will this child be?' For the hand of the Lord was with him."*

As we read in this passage, when Elizabeth and Zechariah named their son, there was much surprise amongst those who knew them. It was custom during this time and to name your child, if not for the parents, then after a relative. That being said, naming John was an act of Elizabeth and Zechariah being obedient to God.

Obedience to God is a foundational part of our walk with Christ. When parents bring their children before the church and congregation, they are doing it out of obedience to God. When Elizabeth and Zechariah named their son John, it was out of obedience to God. When Christ was baptized by John, it was Him showing obedience to the Father. It can be tough to be obedient in our lives; whether it be at work, with parents, teachers, or you fill in the blank. However, it is a foundational part of our walk with Christ that should reverberate throughout every facet of our lives. So, as we dive deeper into this guy named John, his life began with the foundation of obedience from his parents. I challenge you to take a step back and find an area in your life where you need to be more obedient to God.

02 / *Carole Combs,
Wife of Lead Pastor Jim Combs*

Ministry

Ministry

If I ran into you and told you that I had some good news to share with you, would the words "good news" peak your interest? Most people like to hear good news. They like to hear the news that has benefited others and of course, news that will benefit them. What if the supposed good news I shared with you was not good news to your ears at all? What if it even made you angry? The Bible tells us that John the Baptist preached the Good News to the people.

What was the Good News? Do you think John's message was warmly welcomed by all who heard it? _____
_____
_____

Do you like to hear good news? How much more do you like to hear it when it pertains to something good happening to you?
_____
_____

No matter how it was received, John obeyed the call of God on his life to spread the news of repentance. He would be the voice to bear witness and point people to Christ. Everywhere John the Baptist went, his message was met with opposition. Certainly, one would think, why would anyone oppose good news? However, no matter the difficulty or opposition to the ministry that God had called John the Baptist to, he accomplished it.

How do you feel when something you share with others is not well received? _____
_____
_____

What are you first thoughts or actions when someone is in opposition to you? _____
_____
_____

What has God called you to do for Him? Have you obeyed Him yet?
_____
_____
_____

John was living in the wilderness region of Judea. It is likely that he may have been attending sheep because this region was a good place to pasture sheep. His occupation would quickly change when God called him to speak on behalf of the coming Messiah. I know we do not have much of John's life recorded in the Bible before his call from God. Let us imagine for a bit. John the Baptist is comfortable in his sheep business. He can make a comfortable home and have a comfortable lifestyle. Then God calls him to a ministry, and his world is turned upside down. He then has a choice. Do I obey what God has asked me to do? Who is going to take care of my sheep? My business? My home? Should I pretend that God was not talking to me? Or maybe I will obey when it is a more convenient time for me?

We know from God's Word that John immediately obeyed the call from God. His comfortable life would become uncomfortable. It is interesting that in more than one Gospel the writers describe the clothing that John the Baptist wore. I believe this description is important even today for believers. John was the spreader of the Good News; surely he must have worn a three-piece suit with a tie or what about a long white ornate robe? That is what the ministers of the Gospel are supposed to wear, right? John the Baptist wore a garment of camel hair with a black belt cinched around his waist. God knew then and that for centuries people would dictate what the proper "outfit" would be the one that spreads the Gospel. God cared more about John's obedience and willingness to be a servant than what he was wearing. It is the inside that matters, not the outside.

Do you think Christians should wear special clothing to signify they are followers of Christ? Why do you think God described John's clothing in the Gospels? _____
_____
_____

What are some of the difficulties that you face when your lifestyle looks like Jesus? _____
_____
_____

John the Baptist's ministry was to be the voice of the coming Messiah. He would preach repentance because the Kingdom of Heaven was at hand. To be a witness one would have to have seen an event and John would bear witness about the light. In the Gospel of John, John writes that John the Baptist was instructed by the one who sent him. We know God sent him because it was God's plan of redemption. But who instructed John the Baptist? Could it be the same angel of the Lord that spoke and taught his father (Zechariah) and his mother (Elizabeth) about the birth and life of their son (John)? You may wish that you had your personal angel who would come and visit you with instructions. You must remember what God has given to us today. We have the very presence of God living in believers, the Holy Spirit. We also have the very written Word of God, the Bible. We do not have to wander aimlessly wondering what God's ministry is for our lives. We learn that John the Baptist was instructed, but we are instructed as well. Read the Word of God, obey the Spirit of God, and He will direct you to His plan and His work for your life.

John the Baptist pointed anyone who would listen to his message of repentance. Many received his message and were baptized. There were those opposed to his message. I guess it was time to pack up and go back home to the sheep. Not John, he rebuked those that tried to drown out the message. He called them out for being a stumbling block to those that wanted to receive the message. The ministry that you are involved in may not be bringing the accolades that you thought it would bring. Take a moment and remember for whom you are doing it. Are you doing it for the furtherance of the Gospel? Is it to bear witness of what you have already seen Christ do in your life?

Do you look for accolades when you do good things? Why?
_____
_____
_____

John the Baptist's ministry landed him in prison. John did not commit any crime. It was the guilty hearts of sin that wanted to lock up the message of repentance hoping it could be locked away. It will never go away, nor can it ever be locked up. No matter what any government official or law might say, the Gospel is free to all who will believe.

People wanted to know who John the Baptist was. His identity was mistaken to be the Messiah, Elijah, and even a prophet. This was a perfect opportunity for John to exalt himself, on the contrary, John the Baptist humbly said that he was not even worthy to untie the sandal of the one who was coming. He just wanted to be the vessel for the truth. Today we have "ministers of the Gospel" that have quit pointing others to Christ and are pointing people to themselves. I want my life to reflect Christ so much that my identity can be mistaken for His. I want to humbly say, "I am not the Christ, but it is the Christ who saved me and lives in me, and I am not even worthy to untie His sandal."

Would your identity be mistaken for Christ? If not, why not?

_____

_____

_____

What was John the Baptist's message that was so controversial? It is the same message of hope today that has many people still trying to lock it up and discard it out of their lives and out of this world today. His message was repent for the Kingdom of Heaven is at hand. Repent from what? Repent means to express sincere regret or remorse about one's wrongdoing or sin. Repent from a heart of sin. Confess your sins and be baptized in the river Jordan. Romans 3:23 reads that "**all have sinned and fall short of the glory of God.**" The religious crowd came to John the Baptist proclaiming that they knew God because their fathers knew God. It was not being religious that settles your sin debt to God. It is not speaking or dressing good, or grandma's religion that makes you right with God. Any righteousness you or I might have can never make us right before a holy God. There must be a payment for the sin. John the Baptist's Good News is the same Good News for you and me today. John was preaching that Christ was coming. He was the Lamb of God who would pay that penalty of sin for the world, for you and me. John was baptizing with water, but Jesus was coming to baptize with the Holy Spirit. The people had the choice when they heard John the Baptist's message of repentance. Have you found the Messiah? You have the same choice today. Will you repent of your sins and trust that Christ came to earth as the Son of God? Would you trust that He was the perfect sacrificial lamb that would settle the sin debt for all mankind? Ask Him to come into your life and be your Lord and Savior. Is this message Good News to you or not?

Have you personally repented of your sins and trusted God's redemptive plan through His son Jesus? If not, why? If so, write out how you know that you have. _____

_____

_____

John the Baptist chose to obey God's call to the ministry God had prepared for him. It allowed him to see Jesus! What are you missing out on that God has been speaking to you? What is stopping you? Tragically, John the Baptist's life and ministry ended while he was in prison. I can just hear the Father's voice welcoming John to Heaven, "Thank you, John, for your uncompromising obedience to my call upon your life!"

For God so loved the world that He gave...what are you willing to give for what God gave to you? Do you want to see Jesus?

_____

_____

_____

John the Baptist was given instructions by God for the ministry. We have the Bible and the Holy Spirit to lead and teach us. What is your plan to be instructed and follow through with them?

_____

_____

_____

Ministry / Devotion 1

The Messenger

Jill Osmon / *Assistant to the Lead Pastor*

> "In the beginning of the gospel of Jesus Christ, the Son of God. As it is written in Isaiah the prophet, 'Behold, I send my messenger before your face, who will prepare your way, the voice of one crying in the wilderness: 'Prepare the way of the Lord, make his paths straight,' John appeared, baptizing in the wilderness and proclaiming a baptism of repentance for the forgiveness of sins. And all the country of Judea and all Jerusalem were going out to him and were being baptized by him in the river Jordan, confessing their sins. Now John was clothed with camel's hair and wore a leather belt around his waist and ate locusts and wild honey."
> - Mark 1:1-6
>
> "And the child grew and became strong in spirit, and he was in the wilderness until the day of his public appearance to Israel." - Luke 1:80

God chose John the Baptist as His messenger: The one who would point everyone to the Messiah, the one who would baptize Jesus, the one who He formed and shaped for this role. John was the answer to the prophecy in Isaiah 40:3, **"A voice of one calling: 'In the wilderness prepare the way for the LORD; make straight in the desert a highway for our God.'"** He was shaped and created for a purpose. I do not know about you, but that brings me a lot of peace and a lot of joy. I remember growing up and thinking I wanted to be a teacher, for those who know me well now would probably laugh at that idea. I am not a teacher; God did not make me to be a teacher. He gifted me with other talents, and I believe that we are all created with talents and gifts. I think sometimes we are so focused on what we want to do and not what God has equipped us to do. Most importantly, though, is that no matter what He has shaped you to be, we are to use that to point people to Jesus.

> *"Now John was clothed with camel's hair and wore a leather belt around his waist and ate locusts and wild honey."*
> - Mark 1:6

I have heard the saying 'be in the world, but not of it,' and I have always thought of John the Baptist when I have heard this. He dressed weird, ate strange things; he was not part of the world. But I believe this idea has lent Christians an excuse to huddle together and shun the world and in doing so has somehow created a message that we are better because we are separate. I read a blog the other day that talked about this concept and shed some light on it. David Mathis, on the Desiring God website, said this, "Jesus' true followers have not only been crucified to the world, but also raised to new life and sent back in to free others. We have been rescued from the darkness and given the Light not merely to flee the darkness, but to guide our steps as we go back in to rescue others. So let us revise the popular phrase 'in, but not of.' Christians are not of this world, but sent into it. Not of, but sent into."

John the Baptist was given the privilege to go before Jesus, we have the privilege of coming after Jesus and as Mathis said we have been "given the Light not merely to flee the darkness, but to guide our steps as we go back in to rescue others." John the Baptist was actively **"proclaiming a baptism of repentance for the forgiveness of sins."** We are the messengers now; we are to point people to Jesus, not by isolating ourselves but to actively share the Gospel.

Ministry / Devotion 2

Repent

Phil Piasecki / *Worship Leader*

The ministry of John the Baptist is fascinating to examine. He was chosen by God to go before Jesus, minister about Christ, while always pointing people towards the coming Messiah and away from himself. Everything John the Baptist preached was to pave the way for the message that Christ Himself was going to proclaim when His earthly ministry began. First and foremost, John announced the need for the people to repent from their sins.

> *"Repent, for the kingdom of heaven is at hand."* - Matthew 3:2
>
> *"Bear fruit in keeping with repentance."* - Matthew 3:8

Here in Matthew 3, we see two clear examples of John the Baptist telling the crowd and the Pharisees that they need to repent. He understood that true salvation could not be had unless they were willing to repent from their sins. If someone cannot admit that they have a problem they need to be saved from, then they cannot be saved. Just one chapter later in the book of Matthew Jesus Himself would proclaim the same need for repentance to the world.

> *"From that time Jesus began to preach, saying, 'Repent, for the kingdom of heaven is at hand.'"* - Matthew 4:17

Unfortunately, it seems like today many people forget repentance when they talk about giving their life to Christ. Some people think because they have gone to church for a couple of years or were baptized as a child, that it means they are going to Heaven when they die. Many people "give" their life to Christ, but never actually repent of the sins in their life. Repenting involves clearly turning away from your old sinful desires, and begin to walk in the direction of Christ. If someone gives their life to Christ and their actions, desires, and reactions all stay the same, I would guess that true repentance has not taken place. Naturally, when someone gives their life to Christ they do not become perfect; sanctification is a process that takes our entire Christian life. Every day I know I am going to fail, but every day I know I am going to desire to be more like Christ. That desire to be more like Christ is the true fruit of repentance. When someone turns away from their former life and starts their walk with Christ, there will be noticeable differences.

> *"Therefore, if anyone is in Christ, he is a new creation. The old has passed away; behold, the new has come."*
> - 2 Corinthians 5:17

When someone is "in" Christ, they are brand new. That is the beauty of true repentance and giving your life over to Christ. Your old self passes away, and the new you begins to live. Without true repentance, this new creation cannot be born. John the Baptist boldly proclaimed true repentance, and we need to make sure we have honestly heard that proclamation and have properly responded.

Ministry / Devotion 3

Prep Work

Pastor Ryan Story / *Student Pastor*

John the Baptist had very clear orders for his life. Matthew 3:3 says, **"For this is he who was spoken of by the prophet Isaiah when he said, 'The voice of one crying in the wilderness: 'Prepare the way of the Lord; make his paths straight.'"** John's entire life mission was to prepare hearts and minds for the moment when Jesus would start His ministry. John dedicated his life to preparing the way for Jesus. That kind of dedication is admirable. John was bold, John was an outcast, and John never gave up because he knew what he was preparing.

While I write this my son who is a year and a half, and my five-day-old son are both asleep. While I am still called to model and live out what Jesus told me to do in The Great Commission, I feel compelled to make sure that I am preparing the way for my sons' lives similar to what John did for Jesus. Now when John was preparing the way he was announcing that the Kingdom of God had come. While I do not plan on preparing my sons for any sort of Messianic complex, I do plan on doing everything in my ability to make their path is as clear and straight as possible, so they walk the way the Lord wants them to. The way I look at how I should be preparing the way is similar to John. John was willing to live a life of sacrifice, discomfort, and complete devotion to the task of developing the way.

Every Christian has a person in their life that they should be working to help make their paths straight. No Christ follower is ever going to say they want to be a stumbling block in someone's life. So we should all take a moment and pray to find out what things we need to start doing to help straighten someone's path for them to get to God. Imagine how John felt as the Jesus movement started taking off. Imagine all the toil, all the work that John put in would have been well worth it the moment John started seeing people being healed, people being taught, people starting to draw around the One that John was sent to prepare His ministry.

My hope and prayer in my life is that I can pave the way to God so well for my sons that my ceiling will be their floor. I want to help remove every sin I struggle with if it means my sons have a better shot at serving Jesus. I plan on living a life that opens up a path for my boys. Now clearly every parent is going to say that. But as Christians, how often do we focus on making sure we are living our lives to clear the path for our co-workers, friends, or even the random person you walked passed in the grocery store. Take some time today and think about the things you need to start doing to open a path up for those around you.

Ministry / Devotion 4

A Brood of Vipers

Eric Jeffrey / *Children's Director*

> "*But when he saw many of the Pharisees and Sadducees coming to his baptism, he said to them, "You brood of vipers! Who warned you to flee from the wrath to come? Bear fruit in keeping with repentance. And do not presume to say to yourselves, 'We have Abraham as our father,' for I tell you, God is able from these stones to raise up children for Abraham. Even now the axe is laid to the root of the trees. Every tree therefore that does not bear good fruit is cut down and thrown into the fire."* - Matthew 3:7-10

If there were only one word to describe John the Baptist's look, it would probably be "peculiar." And likewise, if we were to choose one word to describe the message he brought, it would most likely be "repentance." The message of repentance is not well received in the world these days, nor was it welcome to a particular set of Jewish leaders. The Sadducees and the Pharisees were the authority spiritually and doctrinally for the Jews and those following Judaism. These men had no problem calling others to repentance, but it seems as John the Baptist pointed out in the passage it was not something they needed or desired. John's call to repentance implied that they were doing wrong, and they needed to stop doing it, and as a brood of vipers they only were concerned with their kingdom, not The Kingdom.

John's message was **"Repent, for the kingdom of heaven is near."** Does this message imply that those who heard it were doing something wrong? Yes, it does. However, it was being announced as an opportunity. John is saying that God is about to do something wonderful, and God did not want them to be heading in the wrong direction when it came. The coming of Christ and the ushering in of the new Kingdom was what was coming for Jews and Gentiles alike. John's message was a call of preparation because things were about to change and repentance is a call to change. The announcement that the Kingdom of Heaven is near was, by implication, to announce that God is near. John was announcing that the long awaited establishment of God's Kingdom on earth is coming and that death shall give way to life, sin shall give way to righteousness, and justice shall prevail.

The Greek word for repentance is μετνοια (metanoia). It means to change the mind or perception. It is a transformative reorientation of the heart where one turns away from sin and heads in the other direction. Repentance allows us to turn away from sin and move toward God and a right relationship with Him. Repentance is an opportunity. Repentance is part of the Good News message, and there is nothing bad about it at all. Individual righteousness is a requirement of the Kingdom, making repentance a necessary preparation for participation in the Kingdom. Repentance affords one the opportunity to be part of the Kingdom.

In ministry, people put you on a particular pedestal where they feel they need to explain their spiritual status with God to me. The most common thing I hear is "yeah, I believe in God" and "yes, I believe in Jesus" or simply "I am a believer." Like I am the one who is going to judge that when the last day comes. I cannot judge their heart, but I can see with confidence whether or not a person's faith is deep or superficial. Because let us be honest Satan "believes." I say that because to see a person's true salvation is to see a repentant heart, not just a statement. Repentance is the other half of the salvation experience. A profession of faith is made (Romans 10:9-10) that is our declaration to God and to the world we are professors of Jesus Christ and His Gospel. The other half of the salvation experience is repentance. There is a renewing or changing of the mind (2 Corinthians 5:17, Romans 12:2). Without this change in the direction of thinking there cannot be a true salvation experience. Now does this mean we will never struggle with sin? Hardly, Paul the finest example of salvation and repentance struggled mightily (Romans 7:14-22) with these things, but he did not view repentance as a stumbling block but rather a gift God affords to followers as a resource to regenerate the mind.

Repentance is the opportunity for anyone to turn away from sin and head in the opposite direction of destruction. Repentance allows believers to renew the mind and alter the ways of thinking to move toward God and a right relationship with Him. In Mark 2:27 Jesus rebukes the Pharisees again as they distort the divine purpose of the Sabbath day. The man was made "first," and then the Sabbath was appointed for him. The Pharisees and Sadducees had again poisoned its intent like a brood of vipers. Repentance was made for people, just like the Sabbath. It is another way God made for us to know the righteousness of our heart and to be able to discern the faith and hearts of others who claim righteousness in Christ. Repentance is an opportunity, not a stumbling block and is part of the Good News message, and there is nothing bad about it at all.

Ministry / Devotion 5

Winnowing Fork

Pastor Tommy Youngquist / *Children's Pastor*

Let me set the stage. Hundreds of people are gathered at the shore of the Jordan River. Imagine: you are meandering through the crowd of people, and John the Baptist calls you to repent of your sins and turn to the Messiah. You find yourself believing what he is telling you, and John baptizes you in the river. Excitement comes over you. The feeling is great! You make your way back to the shore and right after you get done drying off, the same guy utters these words:

> *"I baptize you with water for repentance, but he who is coming after me is mightier than I, whose sandals I am not worthy to carry. He will baptize you with the Holy Spirit and fire. His winnowing fork is in his hand, and he will clear his threshing floor and gather his wheat into the barn, but the chaff he will burn with unquenchable fire."* - Matthew 3:11-12

Then you think to yourself: Winnowing fork? Threshing floor? Chaff? Unquenchable fire?!? What in the world is this guy saying? Did I not just get baptized? But now he is telling me someone is going to baptize me with the Holy Spirit and fire??

I asked myself those questions while reading this portion of Scripture. Let us start with what we do know. The Bible is very clear on how to be saved. John 3:16 covers that. After you have truly believed that Jesus died, was buried, and rose again to pay for your sins, the Bible is clear that your next step is to be baptized. It is a step of obedience. This step tells other people you are now associated with the Messiah, Jesus Christ. The word 'baptism' means 'immersion by water.' Jesus Himself was baptized by going under water, and we are all supposed to imitate Jesus. So, what does John mean when he said, **"He will baptize you with the Holy Spirit and fire?"**

John uses this powerful analogy to prove a point. He is simply saying that he only has the ability to baptize you with water. But the Messiah (who is Jesus) is coming after him and has the actual power to incorporate your soul with the Holy Spirit. When you believe in Jesus, the belief baptizes you in that fire. You take on the Holy Spirit who helps guide you through life so you can live it more abundantly. Then, and only then, when Jesus separates (with his winnowing fork), those who have believed (wheat) from those who have not (chaff), will you be able to withstand the fire that separates the wheat from the chaff. Wheat stays in Heaven and chaff is burnt up with unquenchable fire.

Water baptism is symbolic of being baptized with the Spirit. It is an outward expression of an inward connection to Jesus. So how about it? When life is over, and you stand before God Almighty, is He going to take his winnowing fork and sift you like chaff? Or is he going to gather you like wheat?

Ministry / Devotion 6

Status No

Noble Baird / *Community Center Director*

When I came on staff here at The River in January of 2014, I was given the opportunity to serve one day a week in our community center. From my first "Maintenance Monday" as it was called, I was amazed at everything that went on in the building. At the time, I was working alongside John Rigg who was in charge of our community center. That first day, he walked me around the building and showed me all the different items we had available for the community. From winter jackets and boots, to kitchen appliances and food, it was so awesome to see the donations we had received from those in the church and surrounding area.

In Luke 3, we continue to dive deeper into the life of John and more specifically, into his ministry. Luke writes in Luke 3:10-14,

> *"And the crowds asked him. 'What then shall we do?' And he answered them, 'Whoever has two tunics is to share with him who has none, and whoever has food is to do likewise.' Tax collectors also came to be baptized and said to him, 'Teacher, what shall we do?' And he said to them, 'Collect no more than you are authorized to do.' Soldiers also asked him, 'And we, what shall we do?' And he said to them, 'Do not extort money from anyone by threats or by false accusation, and be content with your wages.'"*

In this passage, John is teaching the people about what it means to really love the community. John was challenging the status quo of the people. He was challenging them not for his personal gain, but so that those who were in need would be loved and comforted.

Fast forward three years and I now have the opportunity to be the Director of the Community Center. It is truly a blessing to be able to reach out into the community and bless them in any way possible. Whether it is by providing some kids with new shoes, a family with food for the week, or simply praying with someone who is struggling; we have been given an incredible opportunity to reach our community. John understood what it meant to love the community and all who lived in it. Not only did he love and want to help the poor, but he also reached out to the rich, the corrupt, and the sick. He did this so that they would understand the love of Christ; who was coming.

You see, John challenged the status quo of his time. He told those who had an abundance to give to those in need; those who were corrupt, to not take more; and those who were in authority, to not abuse it. As followers of Christ, we have been given the opportunity to do the same. Like John, we have been called to love the community we live in and to show Christ's message of love. We cannot simply say give to the community and not do it ourselves. So, will you challenge the status quo as John did? If doing the right thing was easy, everyone would be doing it. Would they not?

03 / *Pastor Trevor Cole*

Imprisonment and Doubt

Imprisonment and Doubt

America. The land of the free and the home of the brave. A nation where we can freely worship the God who created us without fear of persecution. Despite the political tension that seems to anger and divides nearly everyone we talk to, we have more freedom than the vast majority of the world has ever known. We simply have no clue what it would be like to have our very lives threatened for being a follower of Jesus. Millions of people around the world still face that fear, but as Americans, we do not. Because of that, it is difficult for us to relate to what happened to John the Baptist. The man who God called to prepare the way for Jesus lay in prison, persecuted for the very words he could not help but speak.

> Matthew 11:2-3 – *"Now when John heard in prison about the deeds of the Christ, he sent word by his disciples and said to him, 'Are you the one who is to come, or shall we look for another?'"*

Why do you think John the Baptist sent his disciples to Jesus to ask that question? _____
_____

We may not be able to relate to the striking pain of a gouged out eye and certain death just days or hours away, but I believe that John faced something far deeper than physical pain that we can all relate to — Doubt.

Take a look back on your life and recall some of the moments that may have caused you to doubt. _____
_____

How did you handle some of those difficult times of questioning?

_____

_____

_____

For some of us, taking a look back at those moments of doubt was difficult, even painful. For whatever reason, be it our upbringing, cultural norms, church experience, or any number of reasons, we have a tendency to push our doubts below the surface instead of taking the plunge and seeking the answers. I want to challenge you, though, do not run away from that doubt. You have to face it down, or it will certainly return with a vengeance. The world is filled with people who have walked away from Jesus and the church because they would not or could not deal with the doubt that encircled their life.

Following Jesus will often push us to our limits. God wants it that way. It forces us to look to Him instead of just trying to pull ourselves up and do it on our own. If you are anything like me, that in itself poses quite the challenge. I like to take control and just make things happen, but it just does not work that way in our walk with God.

> 2 Corinthians 12:9-10 - *"But he said to me, 'My grace is sufficient for you, for my power is made perfect in weakness.' Therefore I will boast all the more gladly of my weaknesses, so that the power of Christ may rest upon me. For the sake of Christ, then, I am content with weaknesses, insults, hardships, persecutions, and calamities. For when I am weak, then I am strong.'"*

In your own words, how can you be strong when you are at your weakest? _____
_____
_____
_____

It is often easy to focus on the difficult times in our lives instead of all the good, especially in a moment of real hurt and pain. It is important to take stock of all the blessings God has given us as well. As you look back, how have you seen God step into your life in a powerful way? _____
_____
_____
_____

Let's jump back to the answer that Jesus gave to John the Baptist's disciples. Matthew 11:4-6 says,

> *"And Jesus answered them, 'Go and tell John what you hear and see: the blind receive their sight and the lame walk, lepers are cleansed and the deaf hear, and the dead are raised up, and the poor have good news preached to them. And blessed is the one who is not offended by me.'"*

Imagine that a good friend of yours or, for those of you with children, your son or daughter, questions whether Jesus really is the Son of God, the Messiah that He claims to be, how would you respond?
_____
_____
_____
_____

Jesus' answer to John the Baptist sums up the answer to the most important question any of us can ask: "Was Jesus who He said He was?" Jesus reminded John that His life stood as testimony and it must be the same for us. Examine Jesus. What was He like? He is not afraid of us taking a deep look at His life.

It would have been so easy, even understandable for Jesus to simply say something like "that is who I said I was, you can choose to believe me or not." Instead, Jesus looked at those messengers and probably with tear-filled eyes, repeated a prophecy from Isaiah that His life had fulfilled.

Jesus then goes on to say to all the people He was teaching that day in verse 11a: **"Truly, I say to you, among those born of women there has arisen no one greater than John the Baptist."** What an encouragement to know that one of the greatest followers of Jesus faced the same struggle that we all will. It was not just John the Baptist who struggled, though. The pages of the Bible and history are filled with the stories of people who struggled, and we can be sure that we will not be spared. If God and the authors of the Bible were afraid of 'doubt' they could have easily blotted it from the pages of Scripture. No matter how intelligent, focused, and trusting you think you are, this life will bring pain and difficulty which so often leads to doubt. You can choose to ignore it, suppress it and act like it does not exist. But please remember, doubt is a part of faith. As Philip Yancey once said, "Inquisitiveness and questioning are inevitable parts of the life of faith. Where there is certainty, there is no room for faith."

John the Baptist was prepared to lose his life for the cause of Jesus and was eventually beheaded for it. He was not without his questions and struggles, but he continued trusting Jesus. I often ask myself if I would or could follow Jesus in a country that persecuted believers like that. I hope and pray that I will follow Him no matter the cost. Will you? I leave you with the end of the poem "John the Baptist" by John Piper.

> *The dungeon door swung wide, and there:*
> *A soldier in the blinding glare;*
> *And with him stood Herodias.*
> *"We've come to bid you dine with us,"*
> *She said. But John had no desire*
> *To fight. The time for holy fire*
> *was gone. He knelt and pulled away*
> *His hair and bowed his head to pray.*
> *Such is the path that leads to life:*
> *Uncover sin and feel the knife.*
> *The way is lit by candle two.*
> *Who follows John? Jesus! And You?*

Imprisonment and Doubt / Devotion 1

I am not the Christ!

Debbie Kerr / *Office Administrator*

"*And this is the testimony of John, when the Jews sent priests and Levites from Jerusalem to ask him, 'Who are you?' He confessed, and did not deny, but confessed, 'I am not the Christ.'*" - John 1:19-20

Have you ever looked up to a Pastor, Bible teacher, or other religious leader as a replacement for the Word of God? If they said it, it is gospel, even if it is just their opinion or interpretation. This is what started to happen to John the Baptist in John chapter one. We learn a little about John the Baptist in the Gospels, he was known for many things and was gaining popularity among the Jewish people. People started following him, crowds gathered and the people listened. John the Baptist was the cousin of Jesus, it is not clear how far removed they were but the Bible teaches they were related on their mother's side. John the Baptist was a very wild man that lived in the wilderness, wore animal skins and his diet consisted of locusts and honey. He was an interesting character for sure, but God put a special anointing on him because he would be the one chosen to be the front runner to Jesus' earthly ministry. John's message was all about repentance and baptism to prepare the Jewish people for Christ's message and offer of redemption. The Jewish people were excited because they had been waiting for the Prophet Elijah to come to free them from the tyranny of Rome and the religious leaders.

As John taught and baptized, the people became increasingly curious and confused regarding his identity and began inquiring, saying things like, "Are you Elijah the Prophet"? When he denied being Elijah, they asked, "Are you the Christ?" It was then that he revealed his purpose and the introduction to who Jesus was by saying, **"I am not the Christ, I baptize you with water but the One coming after me, He will baptize you with the Holy Spirit and fire."** Shortly after, Jesus arrived on the scene to be baptized, and John said to Jesus, "I need to be baptized by you, why do you come to me?" And Jesus replied, "John, this is the will of my Father." Immediately following the baptism of Jesus, the heavens opened, and they saw the Spirit of God descending like a dove and rested on Jesus, and behold a voice from heaven said, **"This is my beloved Son, with whom I am well pleased"** (Matthew 3:17). John refused to be mistaken for Jesus. He even went on to say that he was not worthy to tie His sandals. He said, **"I must decrease, and He must increase"** (John 3:30).

We need to be the John the Baptist's of our day to the lost and dying world around us. We are not THE Christ, but we are called to be LIKE Christ. We are called to point people to Jesus to live our life in a way that reflects Him, not us! It is often said, "You are the only Jesus some people will ever see."

Is your life reflecting Christ today? Do people see Him when they look at you or hear His grace, kindness, and love in your conversations? Jesus is coming back again one day, and there are still many people that need to know Him as their Savior. Every day we are one day closer to His return.

Imprisonment and Doubt / Devotion 2

Voice of God

Phil Piasecki / *Worship Leader*

In our culture today it seems that everyone is seeking after power and status. In the workplace, it is expected that each employee is trying to climb the corporate ladder, with the goal that they get to be the boss one day. We seek after more money, so that we can have a bigger house and a nicer car, so that when people drive by, they think, "Man that person must be really successful!" Culture tells us to look out for #1, and not to worry about who we may bulldoze in the process of getting to the top. The sad thing is, this is contrary to the example Jesus sets for us in Scripture. I want to preface this by saying that it is not wrong to work hard, do well at your job, and get rewarded for that. The issue is our motivation. Our attitude and our heart need to reflect that of Christ and John the Baptist that we see here in the book of Matthew.

> *"Then Jesus came from Galilee to the Jordan to John, to be baptized by him. John would have prevented him, saying, 'I need to be baptized by you, and do you come to me?' But Jesus answered him, 'Let it be so now, for thus it is fitting for us to fulfill all righteousness.' Then he consented. And when Jesus was baptized, immediately he went up from the water, and behold, the heavens were opened to him, and he saw the Spirit of God descending like a dove and coming to rest on him; and behold, a voice from heaven said, 'This is my beloved Son, with whom I am well pleased.'"* - Matthew 3:13-17

John the Baptist had been paving the way for Christ, waiting for Jesus to appear to him. We see in the Scripture that Jesus comes to John asking him to baptize Him. Can you imagine what must have been going through John's head at this point? He easily could have started thinking "Man, the Savior of the world wants me to baptize Him? I must be pretty incredible." However, instead of becoming proud, John humbles himself explaining to Christ that if anything, he should be baptized by Christ. After this, we see that Christ insists that John baptize Him and he agrees. What happens after John baptizes Christ is incredible, the Spirit of God descends upon Christ, and they hear God speak down to them. When we read this account, we see two people who were willing to humble themselves. Neither John nor Jesus wanted to put themselves in front of the other person. Their attitudes lead to a couple of incredible things happening; they got to see the Holy Spirit move and hear the voice of God. I cannot help but think that if we would humble ourselves more, that we would see God move more in our lives. As believers, we should long to see the Holy Spirit do incredible works, and we should long to hear the voice of God. We see an obvious example in this Scripture that if we humble ourselves before Christ, we can see God do some incredible things.

Imprisonment and Doubt / Devotion 3

True Humility

Pastor Ryan Story / *Student Pastor*

"*True humility is not thinking less of yourself; it is thinking of yourself less.*" - C. S. Lewis

I am not a humble guy. Pride is one of the hardest sins in my life. This has always been a struggle for me. The thing that is ironic to me is that I struggle with both sides of pride, the self-conscious part of pride, and I struggle with the egocentric part of pride. Any given day I can have sinful thoughts that I am the greatest, smartest person on this Earth, to the next day thinking that everything I do is useless and meaningless. That is why I enjoy that quote by Mr. Clive Staples Lewis (bet you did not know his name was Clive) because he can tap into the core of what humility looks like, thinking of ourselves less.

I have enjoyed studying John the Baptist over this last month or so. I try to make sure that I read as much as I can about a Biblical topic before I write. One of John's most famous quotes he ever says is found in John 3:30, where he says, **"He must increase, but I must decrease."** This is one of those common Christian jargon verses we like to throw around and make for some amazing Christian tattoos. But like many things in the Bible, things that have been written, we have lost the true meaning, the real depth of the beauty that John is saying. Sadly, I have to admit, I did not realize that John the Baptist said this in John 3. I feel ashamed to admit this, but when I first started reading, I said to myself, "I thought John 3 was all about Nicodemus and Jesus."

Take today to really, really study a conversation that is had in John 3:25-30. A disciple and a random Jewish man (I am assuming) are having a conversation, and they ask John a question. They even ask it using "Rabbi" (which means Teacher), which is a huge sign of respect in the Jewish culture. The men proceed to listen to John as he waxed eloquent exaltations about Jesus. John was a man with a following. John was thought of as one of the champions of the Jewish nation, Elijah. John was a man who could out-preach the Pharisees. John was a man who knew his place.

John knew who Jesus was, as many reading this do. If we want to begin to think about Jesus as John did we have to answer two paramount questions:
1) What areas of your life do you need to start decreasing?
2) What areas of your life do you need to start letting Jesus increase?

Are you trying to control too much in your life? Are you afraid to give, or serve because you do not know when you would get that time or money back? Are you afraid to ask God how to serve Him because it might not be in your plans? When will you start acting like Jesus and finally stop gossiping, swearing, or talking negatively about someone? When we get to a place where those are the hard questions, we get to a place where John was. John was able to serve God faithfully, boldly, and so counter-culturally that he was used to be the small spark that ignited the Jesus movement. And it came from one simple idea; I am going to humble myself, so Jesus can indeed be seen through my actions.

Imprisonment and Doubt / Devotion 4

Doubt

Danielle Hardenburg / *Nursery & Pre-K Director*

Now when John had heard about the deeds of the Christ, he sent word by his disciples and said to Him, **"Are you the one who is to come, or shall we look for another?"** (Matthew 11:2-3). We all have some expectations. Many of us have high expectations on what we want out of life and who we want to become. We work hard to live up to the expectations that are given to us or to fulfill on our very own. So what do you do when the curve ball comes into your life, and things totally change direction? Or maybe things just do not turn out the way you planned. How do you deal with the issue of disillusionment when the way God works shocks or disappoints your expectations? What do you do with your doubt?

John the Baptist's ministry was a call to repentance. He was the messenger preparing the way. John was the first true prophet in 400 years, and he was also kin to Jesus. John baptized Jesus and saw the Holy Spirit descend on Him. Even as He came down to the Jordan River at Bethany, John proclaimed Jesus as the Messiah in the book of John. But now locked up inside a prison facing death for boldly confronting sin, John was having some doubts. If Jesus was the coming Messiah, why was he locked away instead of preaching and preparing hearts for Him? John was so bold at pointing repented hearts to the Good News of Jesus, and yet his circumstances stirred up doubts if Jesus was the One he knew Him to be. Have you ever been there in the middle of unforeseen circumstances; feeling alone, uncertain, confused and having doubts? Sometimes things just do not add up or make sense. When our world seems to be up-side-down, and doubts arise, you are not alone! Even John, who Jesus said **"Among those born of women there has not risen**

anyone greater than John the Baptist" (Matthew 11:11 NIV); was feeling those very things.

John needed to know Jesus was the Messiah. John had known who Jesus was, but he needed reassurance from Him. He needed to know that even though he was in prison and things were not playing out the way he had envisioned, that there was a bigger picture, he just could not see it. So often in our trials, we cannot see what the Lord is doing. Sometimes we do not see the Lord do the things we think He should be doing. We cannot see the big picture, and in those times we need to do as John did and take our doubt right to Jesus. Jesus did not rebuke John for his question; He gave him reassurance. Rest assured that the Lord knows the big picture and trust He is working all things for the good of those who love Him.

> *"But blessed is the one who trusts in the Lord, whose confidence is in Him. They will be like a tree planted by the water that sends out its roots by the stream. It does not fear when heat comes; its leaves are always green. It has no worries in a year of drought and never fails to bear fruit."*
> - Jeremiah 17:7-8 NIV

Imprisonment and Doubt / Devotion 5

The Red Pill or the Blue one?

Ken Perry / *Assistant to the Reach Pastor*

In 1999 a movie took the Box Office by storm. It spawned a franchise that grossed over 3 billion dollars in revenue worldwide. The basic premise is this: Thomas Anderson is a computer hacker who goes by the name Neo and is considered by Morpheus (the leader of the rebels) to be 'the one,' the one that will save them from ultimate destruction by the sentient machines of *The Matrix*. As the movie progresses, it becomes apparent that many people doubt whether Neo is the one. They have placed their hopes of a future without being controlled by the machines firmly on Neo's shoulders and as time goes on, and he does not overthrow the machines in the time frame they have set in their minds, the question of Neo's ability comes forward. The question of "are you the one?" starts to make it around the ship. They begin to doubt whether they were correct in placing their trust in Neo. They were correct by the way.

Solomon said in Ecclesiastes 1:9 that **"there is nothing new under the sun"** and we see that here because this plot line was played out in reality over 2000 years ago. It is the early part of Jesus' ministry, and John the Baptist has been imprisoned by King Herod for rebuking his sin. Like many people, John was probably confusing Jesus' coming to establish a new kingdom to mean He would spearhead the overthrowing of the Roman government, thereby freeing the Jewish people from the oppression and tyranny of the harsh Romans. To the point, John the Baptist in Matthew 11:3 (NLT) sent his disciples to ask Jesus, **"Are you the Messiah we've been expecting, or should we keep looking for someone else?"** Just as in *The Matrix* movie, they were asking "are you the one?"

Some commentators believe this is John asking the question to help clarify the doubt of his disciples. Others say this is John's frustration of being imprisoned and not being able to do what he was called to do, coupled with the misunderstanding of Jesus' purpose. Either way, we see some real-life doubt creep into the lives of some devoted followers. Have you ever been there? Have you ever started to doubt God? Maybe something you were told, or some promise you claimed but was taking too long to come true made you question whether or not you could trust what Jesus said to you. I know I have.

So, let me share from experience a few verses that can help in these situations.

> Isaiah 55:8 (NLT) says, *"'My thoughts are nothing like your thoughts,' says the Lord. 'And my ways are far beyond anything you could imagine.'"*

Doubt creeps in when expectations are unmet. We need to understand that we cannot fit God into our mold and try to make His plans conform to ours. We must work hard to fit into His plans. Not only are His thought higher than ours, but His timing is also perfect. 2 Peter 3:9a tells us, **"The Lord is not slow to fulfill his promise as some count slowness…"** and Philippians 1:6 (NLT) says that He is faithful to complete the work He started in us. **"And I am certain that God, who began the good work within you, will continue His work until it is finally finished on the day when Christ Jesus returns."**

So, when doubt and fear creep in, when frustration rears its head, when you begin to question whether or not God is hearing your cries and listening to your heart, when you think God's plan for your life is never going to happen, be reassured. Please remember that His plans and purposes are high above ours, His timing is perfect, and the work He began in you will be completed. Stay close to Jesus and do not allow the toothless words of the enemy to cast a shadow of doubt on the greatness of the Word that comes from a Father who loves you dearly.

Imprisonment and Doubt / Devotion 6

Blessed to be a Blessing

Noble Baird / *Community Center Director*

One of my first mission trips I ever went on, was to the streets of Atlanta. Our mission was to help clean at a homeless shelter, then to travel the streets in the afternoon to try and minister to the homeless. During our walks, we took backpacks with supplies such as clothing, food, Bibles, and essentials. We not only wanted to be able to help meet the people's physical needs but also hoped to reach into their spiritual needs. Every person we came in contact with, we offered prayer. Instead of trying to thump them with the Bible, we simply wanted to love on them by meeting their needs and prayer. It was through this time of prayer that we, as a teenage group on a mission trip, were most blessed.

In Matthew 3:4-6, Matthew sheds some light into the physical attributes of John. It reads, ***"Now John wore a garment of camel's hair and a leather belt around his waist, and his food was locusts and wild honey. Then Jerusalem and all Judea and all the region about the Jordan were going out to him, and they were baptized by him in the river Jordan, confessing their sins."*** John was a simple man. He did not have much, nor was his appearance anything that caught one's eye. However, it was through that simple and what some would consider "poor" appearance, that lives were changed.

When I was on the streets asking if I could pray for the homeless, they turned the tables on me. They asked me if they could pray for me! I was dumbfounded and speechless. Our whole goal on the trip was to pray for, be a blessing to, and reach the homeless; yet, they ended up blessing my life. I thought that I was the one who had something to offer. Yet, it was through those men and women on the streets — who had nothing more than the ripped, torn, and dirty clothing on their backs — that I was shown what the actual message of Christ was. John's mission was not to gain followers to his cause. His mission was to spread the message of Christ, through the repentance of sins and baptizing them.

In the culture we live in, we often can let the outward appearance of people bring about a judgment of them. For me, I saw homeless men and women and never once thought that they would have anything to offer me; and I could not have been more wrong. God chose to use a simple man to change the lives of those throughout Jerusalem, Judea, and Jordan. So, as you move forward each day, remember that it is about the message inside; not what the deliverer looks like on the outside.

04 / *Pastor Caleb Combs, Gathering Pastor*

Death

Death... There is nothing I hate more than death. I try and avoid death as much as I can, so much so I am avoiding writing this lesson because I do not want to deal with this topic of death. Confession time: I have credited my lack of time for not writing this lesson (I am way past the due date), but when I saw I was given this assignment I was horrified because I knew I would have to deal with death. Confronting death, whether it is a 96-year-old lady who has lived a full life or the tragic loss of a child, is something for which no one can adequately prepare. I know you might be thinking, "Well are you not a pastor and are you not trained in helping people deal with death?" My answer to that is that no one can prepare for death. People may say, "Well we have had a lot of time" or "we knew this was coming," but these responses still do not take away the pain that death causes. We are going to go on this journey dealing with death together. Please feel free to cry, laugh, or whatever you do in a time of grief as we tackle the heavy issue of death.

Pastor Levi Lusko, author of *Through the Eyes of a Lion, Facing Impossible Pain; Finding Incredible Pain*, writes of the feeling of losing one of his children, "Even when you know your child is in Heaven, it still hurts like Hell."

Who comes to mind whenever you think of death? _____
_____
_____

How do you deal with death? _____
_____
_____

John the Baptist's death was a tragic and sudden death. What started as him confronting Herod for marrying his brother's wife ended with his head on a platter. There are many more details to the story. Read Matthew 14:1-12.

Who was Herodias and what part did she play in the story?

_____

_____

What fear did Herod have? _____

_____

_____

How did John the Baptist die and what were the circumstances for his death? _____

_____

_____

Why do you think Herod grieved over John? _____

_____

_____

> 1 Corinthians 15:26 says, **"The last enemy to be destroyed is death."**

John the Baptist's death resonated all around the Christian world. Jesus described John as the greatest man ever born of a woman, and his life came to a quick conclusion. His death most certainly created fear among many Christians. So we ask the question, "WHY?" This is the most common question asked when it comes to death. "Why did this happen? Why so young? Why didn't I do this or that?" All are valid questions. They are often asked with tears in our eyes and rips in our hearts. We were designed to hate death. Death is our enemy and represents the opposite of Jesus/life. You can ask all the questions you want, but it is not until you grasp the concept of death, and what Jesus did with it, that you can truly deal with it. The apostle Paul gives a great look at death and how we should deal with it.

> 1 Corinthians 15:50-57 says, *"I tell you this, brothers: flesh and blood cannot inherit the kingdom of God, nor does the perishable inherit the imperishable. Behold! I tell you a mystery. We shall not all sleep, but we shall all be changed, in a moment, in the twinkling of an eye, at the last trumpet. For the trumpet will sound, and the dead will be raised imperishable, and we shall be changed. For this perishable body must put on the imperishable, and this mortal body must put on immortality. When the perishable puts on the imperishable, and the mortal puts on immortality, then shall come to pass the saying that is written: "Death is swallowed up in victory." "O death, where is your victory? O death, where is your sting?" The sting of death is sin, and the power of sin is the law. But thanks be to God, who gives us the victory through our Lord Jesus Christ."*

How do these verses give you comfort in death? _____
_____
_____

Where and when did death enter into the world? Hint: Read Romans 5:12-21. _____
_____
_____

> Romans 6:23 says, *"For the wages of sin is death, but the free gift of God is eternal life in Christ Jesus our Lord."*

How does one gain victory over death? _____
_____
_____

> Hebrews 2:14-15 adds, *"Since therefore the children share in flesh and blood, he himself likewise partook of the same things, that through death he might destroy the one who has the power of death, that is, the devil, and deliver all those who through fear of death were subject to lifelong slavery."*
>
> John 5:24 continues the thought, *"Truly, truly, I say to you, whoever hears my word and believes him who sent me has eternal life. He does not come into judgment, but has passed from death to life."*

Jesus, the Son of God, humbled Himself and stepped out of Heaven to become a man. He lived a perfect life and paid our debt by dying on the cross for our sins. The wages for our sin should have been death, not just physical but eternal death, and yet when Christ went to the cross, He paid that wage for us. Because He was sinless, only He was worthy to pay that debt. He took death on Himself and conquered it when He rose from the grave three days later. Death could not hold Him! Acts 2:24 says, **"God raised Him from the dead, freeing Him from the agony of death, because it was impossible for death to keep its hold on Him."** For that, we can be eternally grateful!

We are all going to experience death at one point, and it will never be easy. Even Jesus struggled with physical death. Check out John 11:35 (the shortest verse in the Bible). Here we see Jesus experiencing a similar emotion that we do in dealing with death, **"He wept."** Even though He knew that in a few minutes He would pull off a super sweet miracle and bring Lazarus back to life in a way that would make David Copperfield applaud, He still felt that sting of death. Death may seem like a painful ending, but it does not have to be. Jesus has given us the victory over death, and it does not have to be the finish line. I can tell you there are a few people I look forward to seeing when I walk through the pearly gates, and I am sure there a few you are looking forward to seeing as well. VICTORY sometimes hurts, yet the finish line is going to be incredible. Paul sums it up at the end of his life.

> Philippians 1:19-21 says, *"For I know that through your prayers and the help of the Spirit of Jesus Christ this will turn out for my deliverance, as it is my eager expectation and hope that I will not be at all ashamed, but that with full courage now as always Christ will be honored in my body, whether by life or by death. For to me to live is Christ, and to die is gain."*

Have you received the free gift of eternal life? _____

Who can you pray for who needs to experience victory over death?
_____
_____
_____

Death / Devotion 1

Prophet vs. Politician

Katrina Young / *Nursery & Pre-K Director*

Our country has just gone through a political process that might be considered the most controversial in history. Respectfully, our country has elected a man to the office of the presidency that simply did not fit the mold expected of a political leader. We have a president that did not come through the ranks as one would expect to leave him open to criticism. His legacy remains to be seen, but the uncertainty gives way to protesting, rioting, and confusion. If this is happening in our world today what must it have been like when Jesus walked the earth professing to be "The Messiah"?

Was Jesus who He claimed to be? He certainly did not fit the mold of what people thought He would be. The Bible is filled with Scriptures and prophecies describing who Jesus is, His life and what He came to do. The Jews had expectations of what the "Messiah" would be, but they expected an earthly king. Isaiah 9:6 says, ***"And the government will rest on his Shoulder and his name shall be called Wonderful Counselor, Mighty God, Everlasting Father, Prince of Peace."***

During His ministry on earth Jesus did not deny that He was the fulfillment of prophecy; He spoke very openly about who He was. John 5:39-40 says, ***"You search the Scriptures because you think that in them you have eternal life; and it is they that bear witness about me, yet you refuse to come to me that you may have life."*** The signs and wonders that He performed were merely a testimony to who He was, but His message was salvation and eternal life.

Even today there is controversy about who Jesus was; was He a prophet? According to Scripture? "Yes." After Christ's death and the establishment of the Church, the understanding was that Jesus was the fulfillment of Moses' prophecy. Peter explained that Jesus Christ was the One spoken of by Moses (Acts 3:22-23), *"Moses said, 'The Lord God will raise up for you a prophet like me from your brothers. You shall listen to him in whatever he tells you.'"*

We see this fulfilled in John 3:16, *"For God so loved the world, that he gave his only Son, that whoever believes in him should not perish but have eternal life."* Jesus did not come to govern as a political king; He came to give His life that through His death and resurrection we have the opportunity to receive Him. In receiving Him, He will govern our hearts until His return when He rules the earth as King of King and Lord of Lords.

Instead of skepticism and wonder go to Scripture.

> Jeremiah 29:13 says, *"You will seek me and find me, when you seek me with all your heart."*

Death / Devotion 2

Prompting

Phil Piasecki / *Worship Leader*

In Matthew 14 we find John the Baptist arrested and thrown in jail. Herod had arrested him because John had told Herod that it was not lawful for Herod to have his brother's wife. The story only gets stranger from here as well. At Herod's birthday party he decrees that whatever the daughter of Herodias (Philip's wife) wants, she could have. We see in this next piece of Scripture that Herodias quickly takes advantage of this decree.

> *"Prompted by her mother, she said, 'Give me the head of John the Baptist here on a platter.' And the king was sorry, but because of his oaths and his guests he commanded it to be given. He sent and had John beheaded in the prison, and his head was brought on a platter and given to the girl, and she brought it to her mother."* - Matthew 14:8-11

After being prompted by Herodias, her daughter demands the head of John the Baptist on a platter. The king had no choice but to honor the oath he made in front of all of his party guests, so he commanded the death of John the Baptist. The phrase **"prompted by her mother"** stood out to me in this section. Herodias' daughter allowed her mom to influence her to do something horrible. I am sure most of us find this appalling, but the scary thing is so many of us let this happen in our lives. This story should serve as a warning to the negative influence people can have on our lives.

In my life, I have learned the truth of 1 Corinthians 15:33, **"Do not be deceived: 'Bad company ruins good morals.'"** I have seen it happen in my life, and I have witnessed it ruin the lives of many other people. It is so sad when you see someone who gets wrapped up with the wrong people, and you see their relationship with God slowly disintegrate. When we think of a situation like this, most of us probably think about a student being influenced by his friends at school. However, this issue is something that affects all people in all stages of life. No one, no matter their age, is impervious to the impact their friends have in their life.

> *"Whoever walks with the wise becomes wise, but the companion of fools will suffer harm."* - Proverbs 13:20

We need to surround ourselves with those who are wise, and we need to seek out those people who love God with all their heart. Being around people who are truly on fire for Christ is contagious. This is one of the reasons it is so important to be involved in a gathering and attending a Growth Community. We need to constantly surround ourselves with godly people, allowing them to speak truth into our lives, stirring us up to be more like Christ. This does not mean hide from anyone who is not a Christian. It is essential that in our Christian life we are making friends with people who do not know Jesus. That is the primary way we will have opportunities to share the Gospel of Jesus Christ. We must be diligent to make sure that we are the ones influencing our non-Christian friends and not the other way around.

Death / Devotion 3

A Job Well Done

Pastor Ryan Story / *Student Pastor*

Often we wonder what was going on in someone's head. I recently watched my son head-butt a wall, and I wondered, "What are you thinking?" I have watched teenagers do the most idiotic things, and I stare at them and ask, "What was going through your brain when you thought that was a good idea?" I also try to do this when reading the Bible. What was going through Enoch's mind when God brought him to Heaven? What was going through David's head when Goliath went down? What was going through Peter's mind when he walked on water? Finally, what sort of thoughts were going through John the Baptist's mind right before he was beheaded.

Take some time to read the story of John the Baptist's beheading in Matthew 14. For the gruesomeness of this passage I do not want to go into great detail about this passage, and since anyone from 8- 80 could be reading this devotional, I will have to put a "parental advisory" on verses 8-12 as I continue. I always wondered what was going on in John's mind. He is sitting in prison; he may or may not have been able to hear that his minutes are numbered. I wonder if John felt regret. He stayed committed to the calling God put on his life. John lived a rather odd life of eating insects and wearing uncomfortable clothes, all for God. He devoted his life to preparing the way of the Lord, and he was now in a place where he would not get to see the end result. Now, John was stuck in a room, where eventually a man would come in, murder him, and display his head.

We all have a tendency to look at how a situation ends and define the end as the result of the whole thing. Think of every team that loses in the championship game. The moment the clock hits 00:00 and a team loses, why does everyone throw their entire season out and considered them failures? Atlanta just lost the Super Bowl with a 95% probability of winning with five minutes left in the game. Now that was a great comeback, but Tom Brady being the G.O.A.T. (Greatest Of All Time), does not take anything away from Matt Ryan or Julio Jones. Just because something does not end in what we deem as a "win," does not make it a loss.

Switching gears from football to John the Baptist. John lost his life in prison after faithfully serving God. John boldly preached repentance to a society that did not want to hear him. John stood up to self-righteous religious people that would murder anyone who stood in their way. John was willing to be an odd-ball, just because it was what God commanded him to do. Go back to Matthew 11. While John was in prison, he had doubts. John sent a servant to ask Jesus if he was truly Jesus. Jesus' response was, **"Go and tell John what you hear and see: the blind receive their sight and the lame walk, lepers are cleansed and the deaf hear, and the dead are raised up, and the poor have good news preached to them"** (Matthew 11:4-5). At that moment I think we can see what was going on in John's mind. Yes, John's life was about to end. However, the job that John was tasked with was just starting to take off. The job that John started was about to be finished by Jesus. The Kingdom of God was starting to roll, and God used John to start the momentum. The reality is all of our lives are but a vapor, and we never know when that last moment will be. But in John's case, I feel he was able to move from this life to the next easily knowing that he did a job well done. He finished his race. He fought his fight. He left this world with no regrets. We can learn a lot about our walk with Christ in even the most brutal of stories. So let us take a page out of John the Baptist's book, and go work for Christ. Let us all go live a life that is worthy of hearing, **"Well done, good and faithful servant"** (Matthew 25:21).

Death / Devotion 4

The Compliment

Isaiah Combs / *Worship Leader and Young Adults Director*

I get some nice emails, texts, calls, or Facebook messages (well, they are not always nice). I love the encouragement and the feedback, good or bad. I believe I am exactly where God wants me and I am doing exactly what I am supposed to be doing. I believe God made me to praise, worship, and serve Him. I was not an accident: I was made on purpose for a purpose.

John the Baptist was also made by God for a purpose.

> Mathew 3:1-3 says, "In those days John the Baptist came preaching in the wilderness of Judea, 'Repent, for the kingdom of heaven is at hand.' For this is he who was spoken of by the prophet Isaiah when he said, 'The voice of one crying in the wilderness: Prepare the way of the Lord; make his paths straight.'"

John's purpose, the reason he was born, was to prepare the way of Jesus. I am not going to lie that is a lot of pressure. He was constantly in battles with the Pharisees. He lived in the wilderness, wore camel hair as clothing, and ate locusts (bugs) and wild honey as food. I just picture John the Baptist to be this man who dressed crazy, did crazy things, and talked crazy (and people complain about Pastor Jim's beard and appearance). Regardless of all these things his ministry grew and grew.

Then one day Jesus shows up, and John's ministry begins to shrink drastically. John's disciples began to complain. They have concerns with Jesus and the lack of people coming to learn from John. He then is quoted in John 3:27- 30,

> *"John answered, 'A person cannot receive even one thing unless it is given him from heaven. You yourselves bear me witness, that I said, 'I am not the Christ, but I have been sent before him.' The one who has the bride is the bridegroom. The friend of the bridegroom, who stands and hears him, rejoices greatly at the bridegroom's voice. Therefore this joy of mine is now complete. <u>He must increase, but I must decrease.</u>'"*

John the Baptist got it. It was not about him or the great things he was able to do. It was all about Jesus.

> Matthew 11:11 adds, *"Truly, I say to you, among those born of women there has arisen no one greater than John the Baptist. Yet the one who is least in the kingdom of heaven is greater than he."*

Jesus pays John the Baptist the greatest compliment a man can receive. He is the greatest man ever born. John decreased himself and made his life all about Jesus.

I am thankful for the compliments I receive from texts, emails, calls, and Facebook. But I want greatness that comes from only Jesus. I must decrease myself and make it all about, for, and because of Jesus.

He must increase.

> Mathew 23:12 (NIV) says, *"For those who exalt themselves will be humbled, and those who humble themselves will be exalted."*

Become the least, and you will be the greatest.

Death / Devotion 5

"Listen to my Mouth"

Holly Boston / *Women's Ministry Director*

When my daughter Mackenzie was four years old, she loved to talk non-stop. She talked from the moment she opened her eyes in the morning until she closed them at night. That was a tough season. Truth be known, she exhausted me. After a while, all I heard was the sound of her voice (much like Charlie Brown's teacher; "Wha, wha, wha...") and I would just give any answer to quiet her. Mackenzie, being intelligent like her mother, realized I was not actually listening and would shout: "Listen to my mouth!"

As I read my assigned verses on John the Baptist, my attention kept turning to Matthew 11:15: ***"He who has ears to hear, let him hear."*** I discovered that Jesus repeated this two other times in Isaiah 40:3 and Malachi 4:5-6. And as we all know, when Jesus repeats Himself, we need to LISTEN. John the Baptist was the last and the greatest of the prophets. He was THE prophet who would announce the long awaited Messiah. It occurred to me that much like Mackenzie wanted to be heard, John the Baptist wanted/needed to be heard. Or did he?

Webster defines hearing as perceiving with the ear the sound made by someone or something. Listen is described as giving one's attention to someone or something. However, actively listening is the practice of paying close attention to a speaker and asking questions to ensure full comprehension. These different "levels" of hearing require various levels of attention and effort. Have you ever heard someone say: "You need to put on your spiritual ears?" Spiritual listening takes hearing to a whole new level. James 1:22 says: ***"Do not merely listen to the word and so deceive yourselves. Do***

what it says." I believe this is the type of listening John the Baptist prayed/hoped for whenever he shouted: ***"Repent, for the Kingdom of Heaven is at hand"*** (Matthew 3:2). And frankly, this is what Mackenzie had hoped. Not just hearing, not just understanding, but responding.

In John 4, we find an excellent example of spiritual listening when the woman at the well encounters Jesus. To begin with, we see Jesus speaking to this Samaritan woman. Culturally this was totally frowned upon and could have caused trouble for both of them. The woman chooses to listen to Jesus' words. Initially, she lacks understanding. She believes Jesus is offering her water and a way to avoid the inconvenience of the well. She pursues understanding by continuing to ask questions and by the end of the conversation she understands who Jesus is and the magnitude of what He is offering: living water, eternal life. After hearing and understanding, she responds by going home and telling all who would listen about her Jesus (John 4:28-30).

This is the spiritual listening God demands of all who believe. We are called to hear the Word of God, understand the Word of God, and share what we have experienced with all who will listen.

I wonder how many times John the Baptist wanted to yell: "Listen to my mouth!"

Death / Devotion 6

Swimming Lesson

Brett Eberle / *Production Director*

My prayer life often leaves something to be desired. I struggle remembering that God wants us to ask, even for the small things. A short time ago God reminded me of that truth, and it prompted me to write this.

I got a few days off and got the chance to go up north fishing with some close friends. One of the guys lost his prescription sunglasses, and we began looking anywhere and everywhere we possibly could to try to find them. After about half the day of searching, I said a quick prayer just asking God to do something cool and help us find his glasses. Literally, within minutes he found the glasses and I thought "wow that was cool" and then just forgot about it as the day went on.

Later that night I was making the drive from where we were fishing to my parents' cabin when I saw red and blue flashing lights in my rearview mirror. I knew I was speeding and knew this was going to be another ticket on my record that leaves something to be desired. The officer was very polite, and I tried to be as I fought off my annoyance with myself for speeding when I know better. He went back to his car to run all of my information, and while I was sitting there, I thought about how great it was to have a couple of days off and that this ticket was going to be the blemish on the whole time. For the second time that day I said a quick prayer telling God that I knew the ticket was my fault but that it sure would be awesome if I did not get one. About that time the officer came back, handed me my cards, and my paperwork and told me to slow down but never gave me a ticket.

While I was continuing the drive to my cabin, I asked why in the world God would do these things for me, a guy who screws up multiple times a day. That was when a small voice inside of me said "I reached down for Peter, even though he could swim" (Matthew 14:22-33). Peter spent his whole life on the water, he would have been an excellent swimmer, but Jesus still reached down to lift him out of the water. Just because you are not drowning in this world does not mean that you should not grab hold of the hand Jesus is holding out for you.

Through my life, I had wondered if or when God was going to tell me that enough is enough and that He is done helping me until I clean up my act. Let us be honest God has done plenty of huge things for us. He sent his only Son so that we could have a way to get to Heaven, He pulled me out of an enormous self-inflicted mess, and He gave me my dream job working at a Church.

When you look at your life, and you see the big things God has done, like letting Peter walk on water, it is easy to forget the little things He does, like reaching down to pick somebody up who could already swim. Do not wade your way through life, grab hold of Jesus' hand and walk on water with Him!

NOTES

- Hunting safety
- Linda (mom)
- Tom unspoken
- Bark - heart
-

NOTES

NOTES

NOTES

NOTES

NOTES

NOTES

NOTES

NOTES

OUR MISSION

Matthew 28:19-20: **"Go therefore and make disciples of all nations, baptizing them in the name of the Father and of the Son and of the Holy Spirit, teaching them to observe all that I have commanded you. And behold, I am with you always, to the end of the age."**

REACH

At The River Church, you will often hear the phrase, "we don't go to church, we are the Church." We believe that as God's people, our primary purpose and goal is to go out and make disciples of Jesus Christ. We encourage you to reach the world in your local communities.

GATHER

Weekend Gatherings at The River Church are all about Jesus, through singing, giving, serving, baptizing, taking the Lord's Supper, and participating in messages that are all about Jesus and bringing glory to Him. We know that when followers of Christ gather together in unity, it's not only a refresher it's bringing life-change.

GROW

Our Growth Communities are designed to mirror the early church in Acts as having "all things in common." They are smaller collections of believers who spend time together studying the word, knowing and caring for one another relationally, and learning to increase their commitment to Christ by holding one another accountable.

The River Church
8393 E. Holly Rd. Holly, MI 48442
theriverchurch.cc • info@theriverchurch.cc

BOOKS BY THE RIVER CHURCH

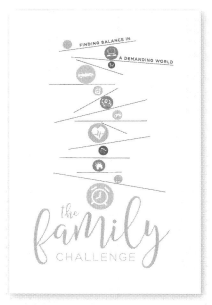

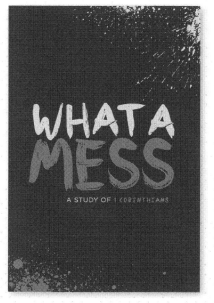

Made in the USA
Lexington, KY
25 September 2017